English Activity Book

for ages 4-5

This CGP book is packed with bright and colourful English activities for children in Reception.

It's a brilliant way to introduce the essential skills — and it's stacks of fun too!

Hints for Helpers

- This book contains practice for **reading** (phonics and comprehension) and **writing**. You can help your child by **reading out the instructions** and **encouraging** them to **sound out** letters and words.

- This book is designed to be worked through in **order**. However, the 'Rob the robot' activity in the centre uses content from **throughout the book**. You may want to complete this activity **last**.

Reading

- The phonics activities in this book cover **Phase Three** of most **systematic synthetic phonics programmes**. The activities are designed to help children practise common sounds and recognise the letters that are usually used to write these sounds.

- Children should practise reading unfamiliar words by **segmenting** them into individual sounds, then **blending** the sounds together to read the whole word.

- For example, to read the word 'sat', they should **segment** the word into separate sounds — 's', 'a' and 't', which sound like 'ss', 'a' and 'tuh'. They should then **blend** these letter sounds together ('ss-a-tuh') to say the word.

- A sound can sometimes be written using **more than one letter**, such as 'ai' in 'r<u>ai</u>n'. These sounds are underlined.

- It is often helpful to use **letter sounds** with your child, rather than **letter names**. For example, if you see the letter 'b', you should say 'buh', not 'bee'.

- Some comprehension questions are **image-based** to help your child practise basic **comprehension skills** before progressing onto **word-based** questions.

Writing

- It's worth noting that every school has its own **handwriting style**. Some schools may form letters differently to how they're written here.

- In this book, some of the letters have **flicks** at the bottom in preparation for **joined-up writing**. Check to see how these letters are written in school.

- For each letter, there is a **red dot** showing where to start. When a new letter is introduced, there are **arrows** to follow.

- You should also encourage your child to hold their pencil correctly, using **three fingers** to manoeuvre it. This is called a '**tripod grip**'.

Contents

j, v, w, x and y	2
z, zz, qu, ch and sh	4
th, ng, ai, ee and igh	6
oa, oo, ar, or and ur	8
ow, oi, ear, air, er and ure	10
Words and sentences	12
Understanding stories	14
Rob the robot	16
What happens next?	18
Sounds and rhymes	20
c, o, a, d and g	22
h, i, j, l and t	24
e, s and f	26
b, u, y, k and q	28
r, n, m and p	30
v, w, x and z	32
The alphabet	34

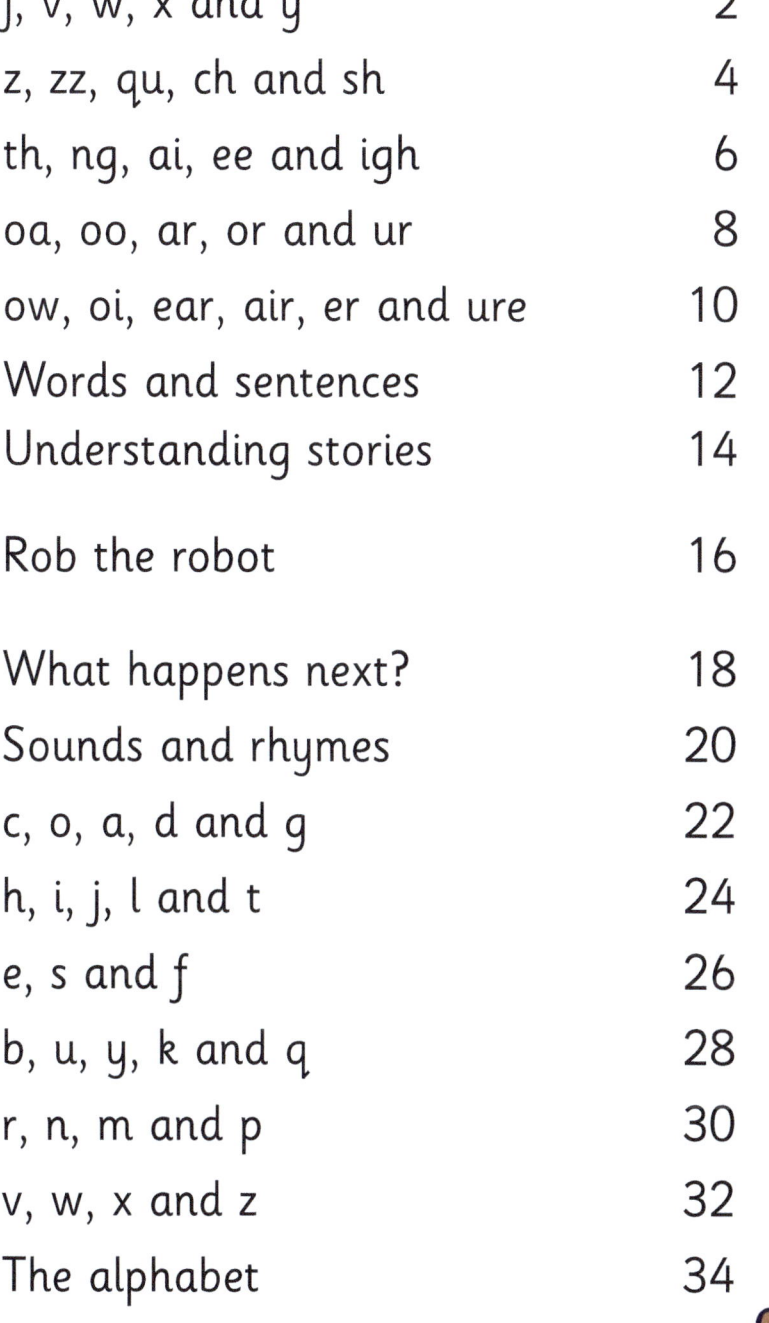

Published by CGP

Editors: Andy Cashmore, Robbie Driscoll, Kirsty Sweetman

With thanks to Rachel Craig-McFeely and Sharon Gulliver for the proofreading.

With thanks to Jan Greenway for the copyright research.

ISBN: 978 1 78908 884 7

Printed by Elanders Ltd, Newcastle upon Tyne.
Cover and graphics used throughout the book © Educlips
Cover design concept by emc design ltd.

Text, design, layout and original illustrations
© Coordination Group Publications Ltd. (CGP) 2022
All rights reserved.

Photocopying this book is not permitted, even if you have a CLA licence.
Extra copies are available from CGP with next day delivery • 0800 1712 712 • www.cgpbooks.co.uk

j, v, w, x and y

How It Works

Practise saying the **j**, **v**, **w**, **x** and **y** sounds.

jump

vet

wag

bo**x**

yell

Now Try These

Draw a circle around two things that start with the **w** sound.

Put a tick under the animal that ends with the **x** sound.

Which sound is missing from the word below?
Circle the right sound.

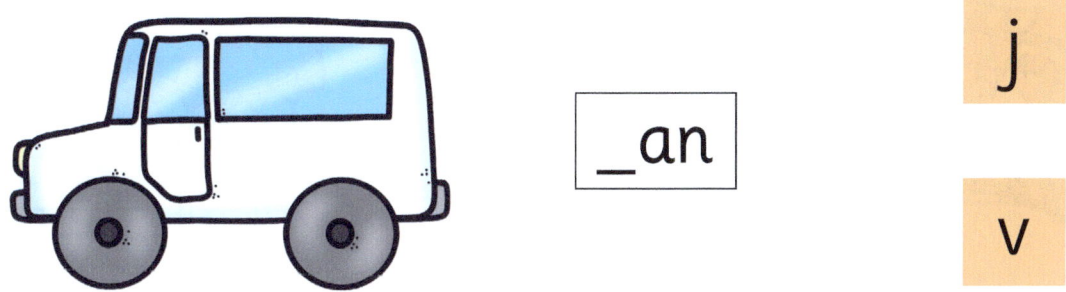

j

v

Draw lines to match each picture to the sound it starts with.

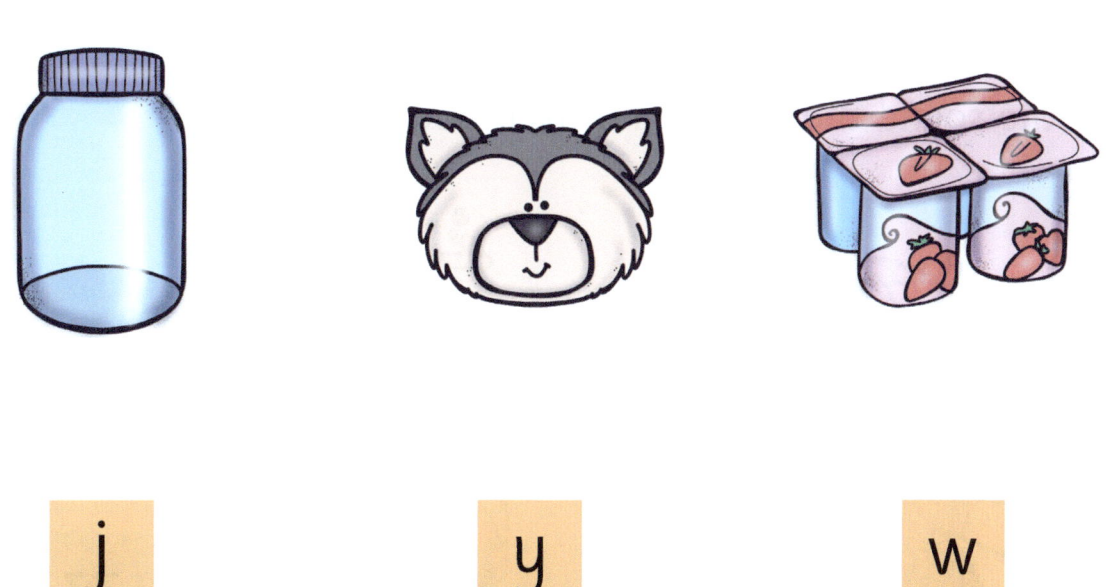

You took good care of those pages! Tick the box.

z, zz, qu, ch and sh

How It Works

Try saying the **z**, **zz**, **qu**, **ch** and **sh** sounds.

z and **zz** make the same sound.

zz only appears in the middle or at the end of a word — never at the start.

zap   bu**zz**

quilt   **ch**in   **sh**op

Now Try These

Circle the sound that is missing from both words.

di__y   fi__y

ch

zz

Circle the picture that starts with the **z** sound.

Colour the foods that start with the **ch** sound.

Draw lines to match each picture to the sound it starts with.

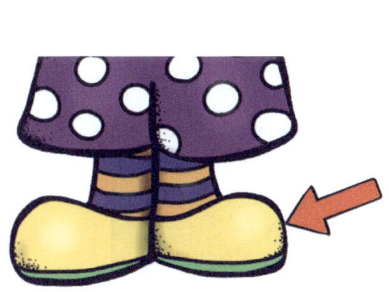  

qu   sh   z

Good job with those tricky sounds! Tick the box.

th, ng, ai, ee and igh

How It Works

Practise saying the **th**, **ng**, **ai**, **ee** and **igh** sounds.

mo**th**

lo**ng**

ng and **igh** only appear in the middle or at the end of a word — never at the start.

tr**ai**n

ch**ee**k

n**igh**t

Now Try These

Colour in the animal that contains the **ee** sound.

Put a tick under the picture that starts with the **th** sound.

Circle the letters that are missing from the word below.

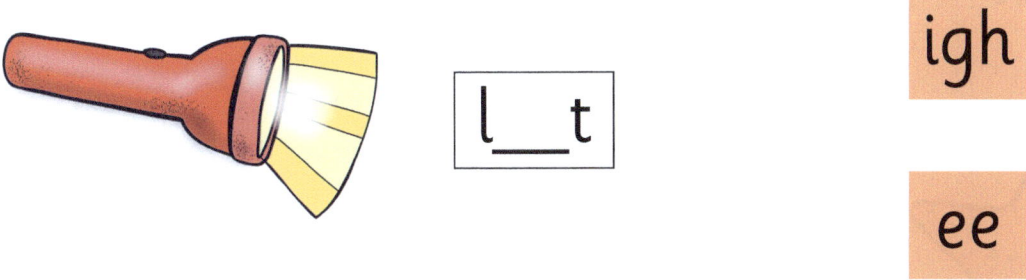

Can you work out what should go in each climber's backpack? Match the things that contain **ai** or **ng** sounds to the correct bag.

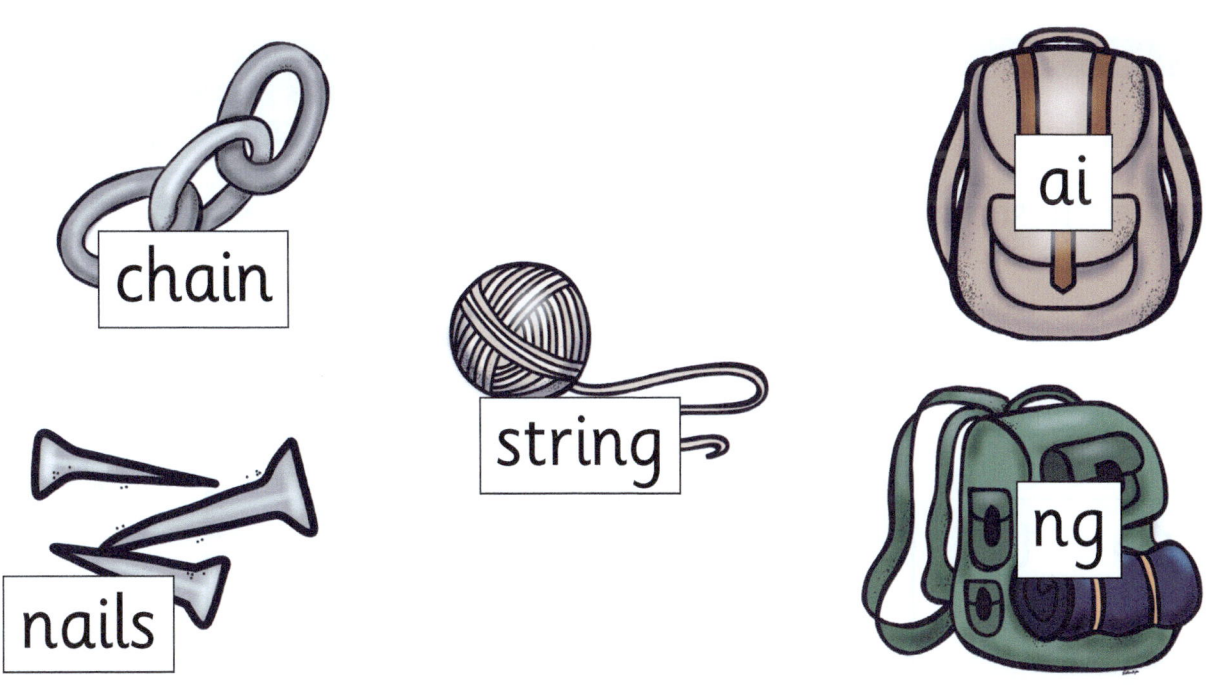

You're at the peak of your powers! Tick the box.

oa, oo, ar, or and ur

How It Works

Practise saying the **oa**, **oo**, **ar**, **or** and **ur** sounds.

fl**oa**t

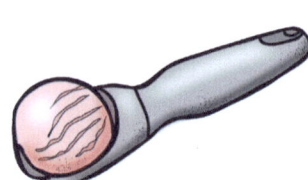
sc**oo**p

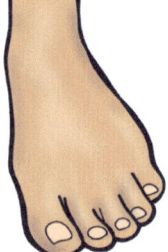
f**oo**t

There are **two** ways of saying **oo**.

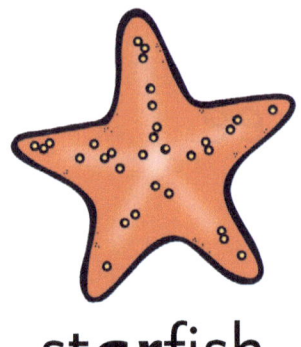
st**ar**fish

c**or**k

b**ur**n

Now Try These

Circle the sound that is missing from the word below.

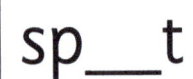
sp__t

oa

or

Circle the picture that contains the **oo** sound.

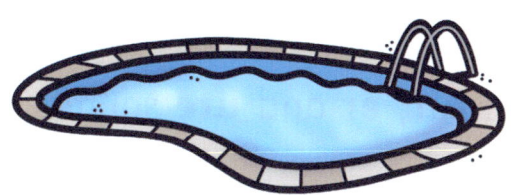 

Colour the thing in the picture that contains the **oa** sound.

Say each of the words below out loud.
Draw lines to match each word to the sound it contains.

  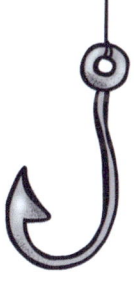

shark   surf   hook

ur   oo   ar

Wow! You really made waves there! Tick the box.

ow, oi, ear, air, er and ure

How It Works

Have a go at saying the **ow**, **oi**, **ear**, **air**, **er** and **ure** sounds.

g**ow**n   p**oi**nt   t**ear**

h**air**   lett**er**   p**ure**

Now Try These

Draw lines to match each word to the sound it contains.

beard

crown

ow   ear

Colour the **two** pictures that end with the **er** sound.

Circle the sound that is missing from the word below.

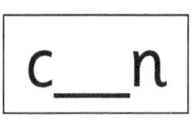 

Draw lines to match each word to the sound it contains.

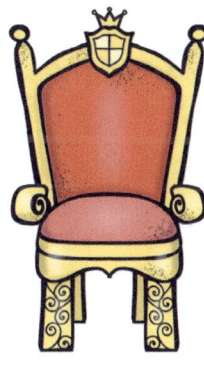   

chair   secure

               air

Congratulations! You did a royal job with those sounds.

 # Words and sentences

How It Works

Have a go at blending sounds together to make words.
Break a word down into its different sounds.
Then, blend them together to say the whole word.

c - oo - k  cook

A sentence is made up of lots of words in a row.

Now Try These

Circle the picture that matches each word.

jam

nut

 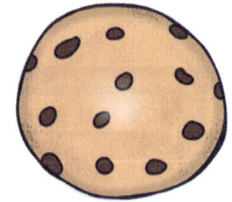    

Draw lines to match each word to the right picture.

eggs   mix   butter

Circle the word that completes this sentence to make it match the picture.

The hat is ___ .

big

red

Colour the picture that matches the sentence.

She is a star cook.

Tick the sentence that matches the picture.

The pan is hot. ☐

It is a fork. ☐

Those pages are done and crusted! Tick the box. ☐

Understanding stories

How It Works

When you read a story, you learn about the characters and what they are doing.

In this story, the characters are called Tim and Meg.

They are looking at some fish.

Now Try These

Look at the picture below and answer the question.

Colour in what the divers have found.

Read the speech bubbles below and answer the questions.

Draw lines to match each picture to the character's name.

Jez

Kim

Where are Kim and Jez? Put a tick under the right picture.

You made a splash on those pages! Tick the box.

Rob the robot

The pictures show Rob the robot's day at work. Put a tick next to the sentence that shows what is happening in each picture.

1

Rob is off to his job. ☐

Rob is in a wood. ☐

Rob needs to fix a car. ☐

Rob has a long nap. ☐

2

3

His drill is in his bag. ☐

His drill is not in the box. ☐

④

He gets help from Bot. ☐

He looks for it by himself. ☐

⑤

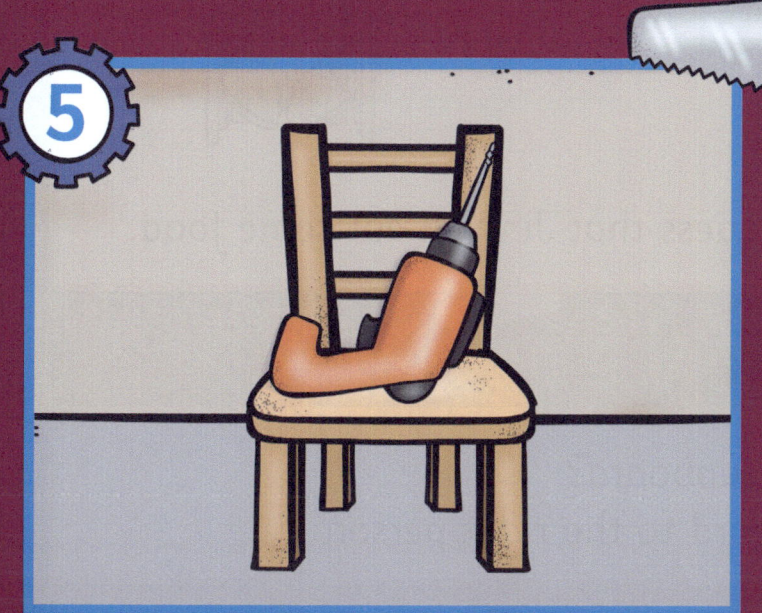

The drill is in the desk. ☐

The drill is on the chair. ☐

Look at the sentences. Tick the sentence that shows what you think will happen next. Draw a picture to match the sentence.

Rob drills the car door. ☐

Rob runs to the shop. ☐

⑥

What happens next?

How It Works

Sometimes when you read a story, you might be able to guess what's going to happen next.

It is time for lunch, so you can guess that Jin will eat some food.

Now Try These

Who do you think will use this cupboard?
Draw a line to match the cupboard to the right person.

Rose is looking for a quiet place to read her book. Look at the pictures below. Where do you think Rose will go to read her book? Tick the right picture.

Read the speech bubble. What do you think will happen next? Draw a line to match the boy to the right picture.

It is raining.

Well done! You taught those pages a lesson! Tick the box.

Sounds and rhymes

How It Works

Some words **start** with the same sound. Practise saying these words.

best **b**ox<u>er</u>   **h**ard **h**it

Some words **end** with the same sound. These words **rhyme**.

w**in**   sp**in**   gr**in**

Now Try These

Circle the picture where both words start with the same sound.

br<u>own</u> box   lo<u>ng</u> jump

Complete these phrases by drawing lines to match the words that start with the same sound.

 tennis   socks

 sports   top

Say these words out loud. Does each pair of things rhyme? Tick the ones that do.

run   sun

swim   shorts

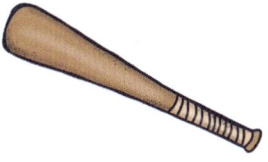 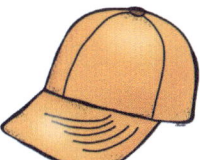
bat   hat

Amazing! You deserve a gold medal. Tick the box.

c, o, a, d and g

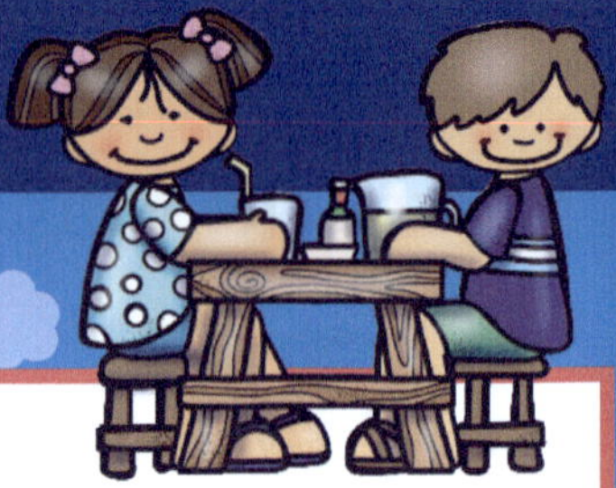

How It Works

These letters all start with a curve.
Start at the red dots and follow the arrows to trace the letters.

c o a d g

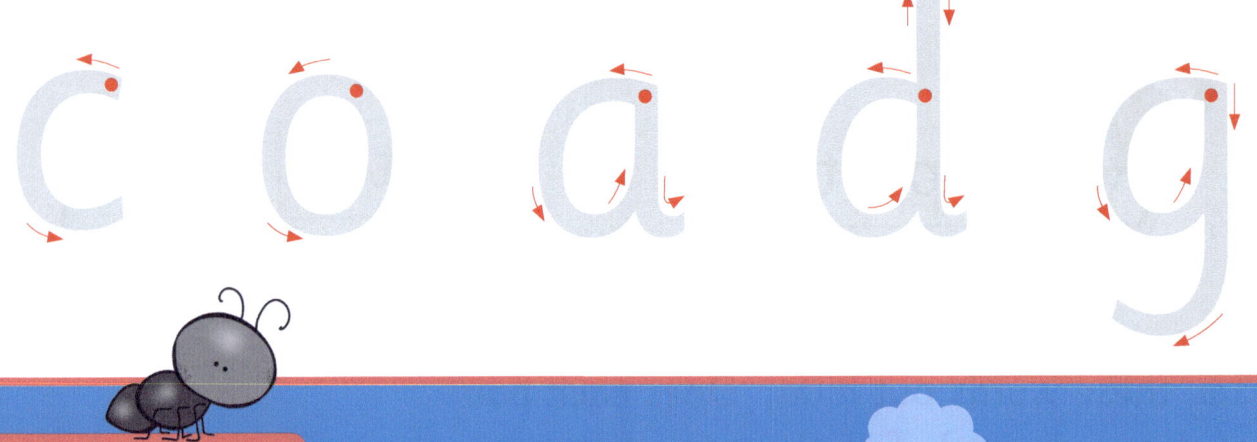

Now Try These

Practise writing the letters below.

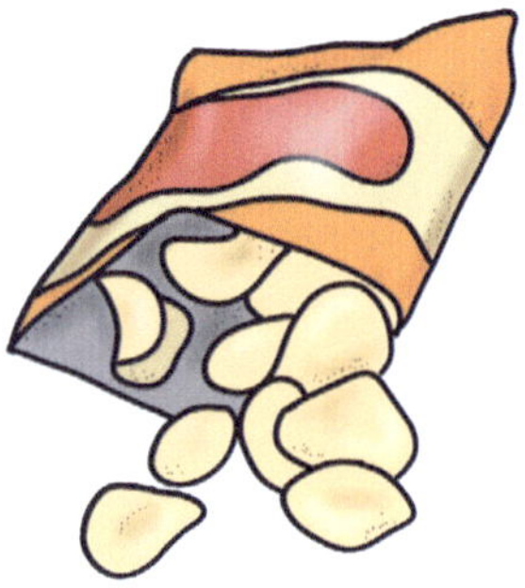

c c c c c

o o o o o

a a a a a

d d d d d

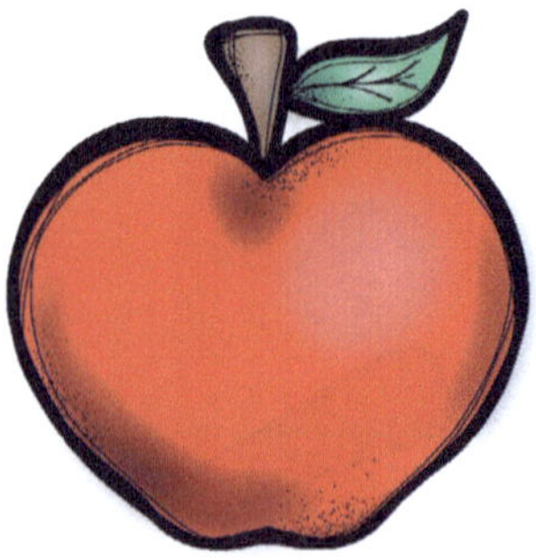

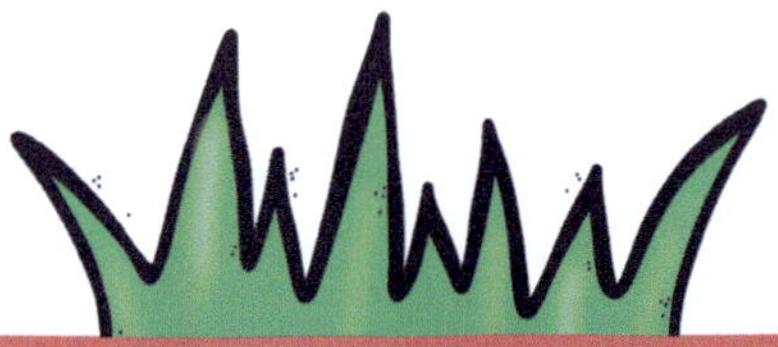

g g g g g

Fill in the missing letters for these words.

picnic

log   salad

Fill in the missing letters, then finish colouring in the picture.

corn   bread

grapes

Great job on finishing those curves! Tick the box.

h, i, j, l and t

How It Works

These letters all start with a straight line and then have a curve. Try tracing these letters, following the arrows.

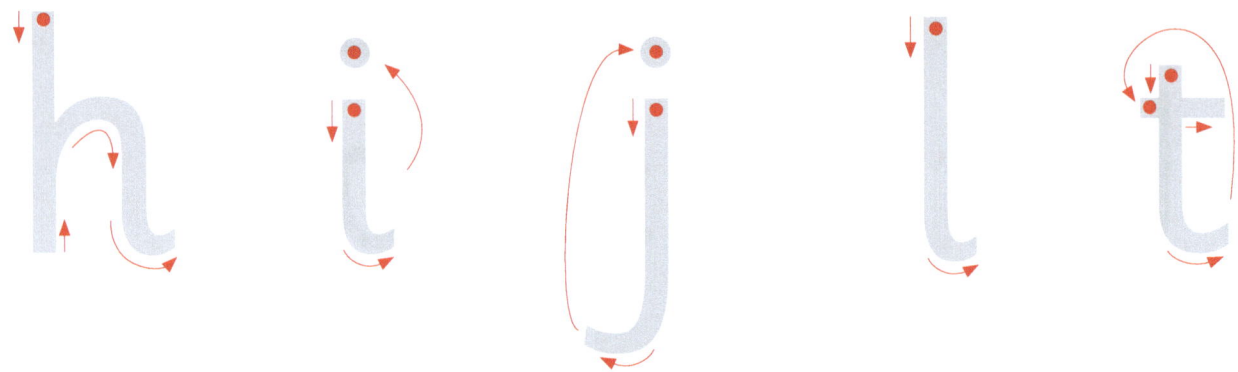

Now Try These

Practise writing the letters below.

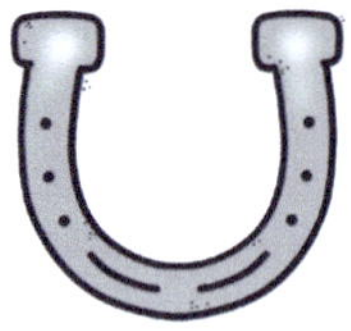

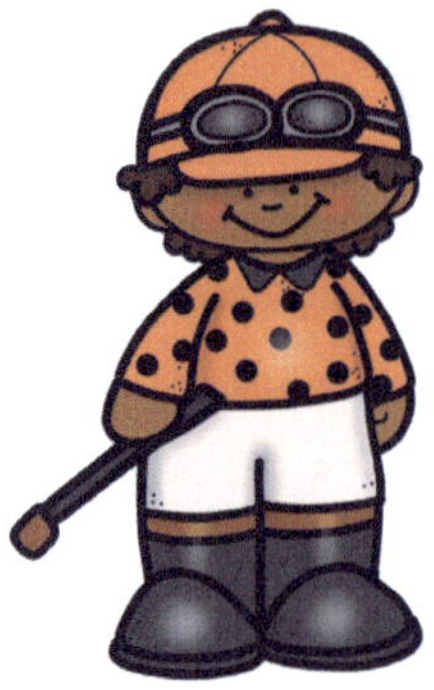

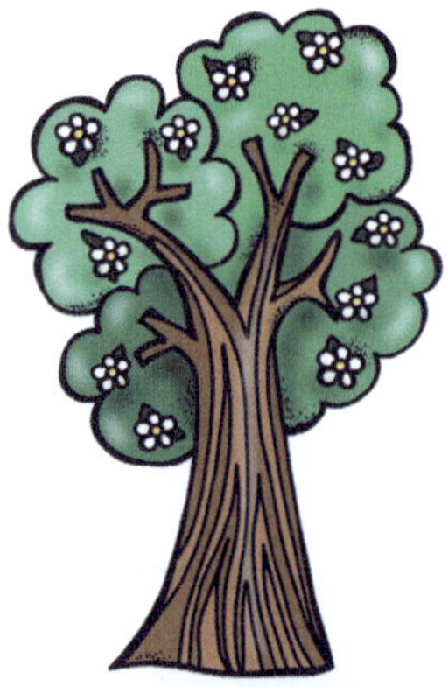

Fill in the missing letters for these words.

jump

high

tall

Fill in the missing letters, then circle all the horses in the picture.

horse

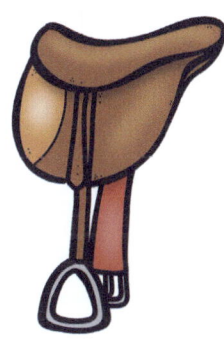

trail

job

Neigh! Nice work on those pages! Tick the box.

e, s and f

How It Works

These letters are all curly.
Follow the arrows to trace the letters.

  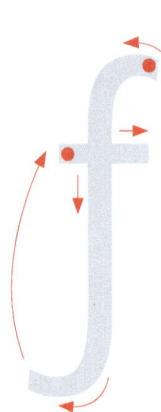 

Now Try These

Practise writing the letters below.

 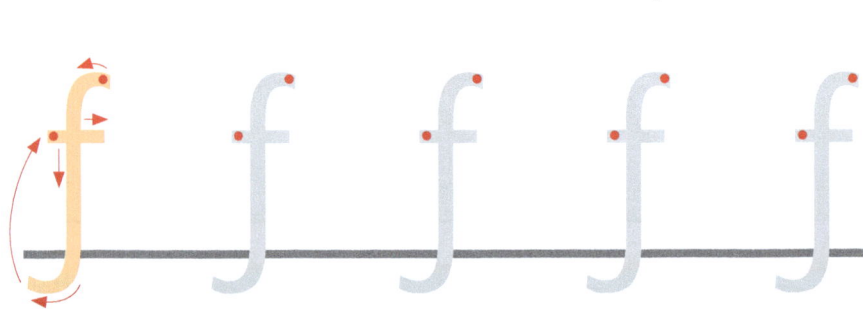

Fill in the missing letters for these words.

star

fly

alien

Fill in the missing letters, then finish colouring in the picture.

far

space

sun

Well done — that was out of this world! Tick the box.

b, u, y, k and q

How It Works

These letters all have straight lines and curves.
Practise tracing these letters, following the arrows.

Now Try These

Practise writing the letters below.

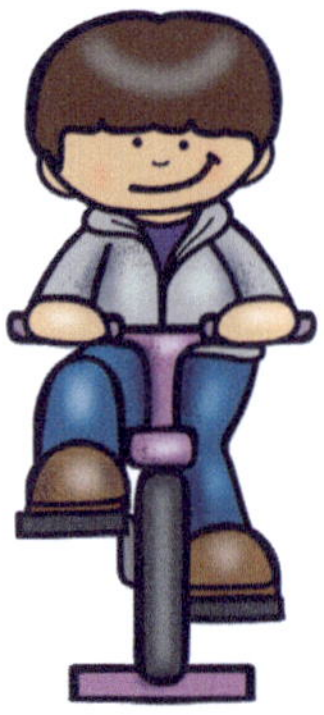

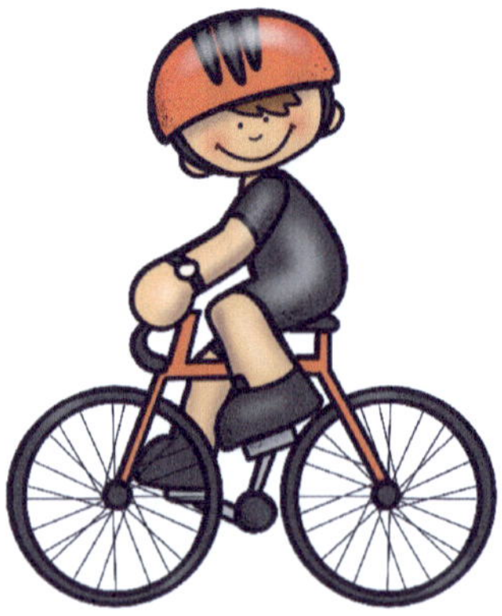

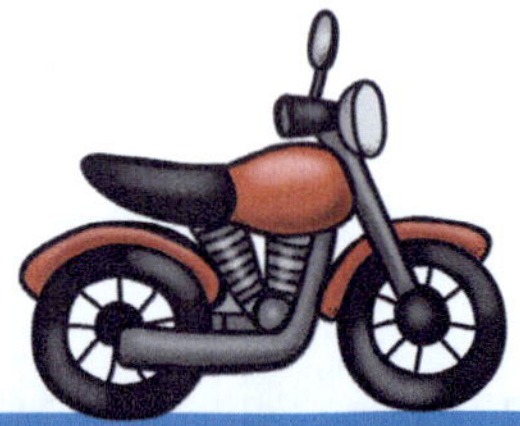

Fill in the missing letters for these words.

bike

cycle

quick

Fill in the missing letters, then circle all the bikes in the picture.

quit

brake

tyre

You whizzed through those letters! Tick the box.

r, n, m and p

How It Works

These letters all start with a straight line. They go down, then back up and over. Start at the red dots and follow the arrows.

 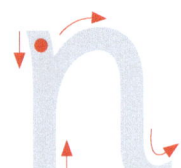  

Now Try These

Practise writing the letters below.

 r r r r r

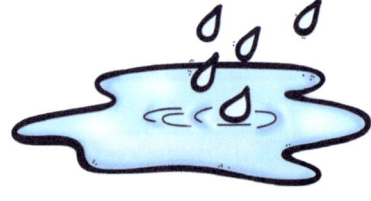 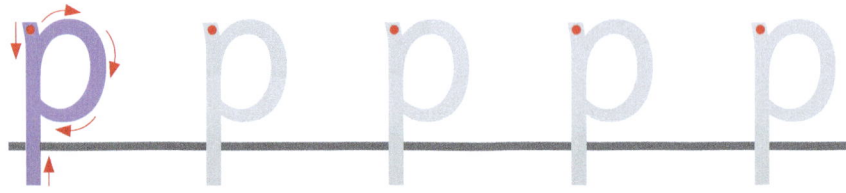

30

Fill in the missing letters for these words.

sun

warm

spring

Fill in the missing letters, then finish colouring in the picture.

rain

drop

mud

You made that look like a breeze! Tick the box.

v, w, x and z

How It Works

These letters are all pointy.
Follow the arrows to trace the letters.

 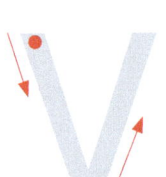  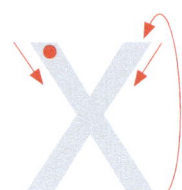 

Now Try These

Practise writing the letters below.

Fill in the missing letters for these words.

hive   wood

   axe

doze

Fill in the missing letters, then finish colouring in the picture.

cave   owl

   buzz

fox

Good job on those pointy letters! Tick the box.

The alphabet

Have a go at writing all the letters in the alphabet. Then, colour in the pictures of the dinosaurs.

a b c d e

f g h i j

k l m n o

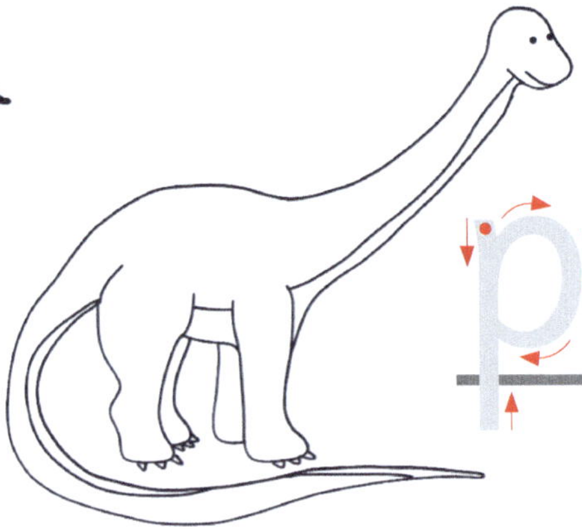

p q r s t

u v w x y z

Roar! Well done on writing the alphabet! Tick the box.